'Twas the Night Before Christmas

Illustrations copyright © 1994 by Mike Artell

All rights reserved. No part of this book may be reproduced or transmitted in any form or by any means, electronic or mechanical, including photocopying, recording, or by any information storage and retrieval system, without permission in writing from the Publisher.

Aladdin Books
Macmillan Publishing Company
866 Third Avenue
New York, NY 10022

Maxwell Macmillan Canada, Inc.
4200 Eglinton Avenue East
Suite 200
Don Mills, Ontario M3C 3N1

Macmillan Publishing Company is part of the Maxwell Communication Group of Companies.

First Aladdin Books edition 1994
Printed in the United States of America

10   9   8   7   6   5   4   3   2   1

Library of Congress Cataloging-in-Publication Data
Moore, Clement Clarke, 1779–1863
[Night before Christmas]
'Twas the night before Christmas / illustrated by Mike Artell.   —1st ed.
p.   cm.
Summary: The well-known poem about an important Christmas Eve visitor.
ISBN 0-689-71801-2
1. Santa Claus—Juvenile poetry. 2. Christmas—Juvenile poetry. 3. Children's poetry, American.
[1. Santa Claus—Poetry. 2. Christmas—Poetry. 3. American poetry. 4. Narrative poetry.] I. Artell, Mike, ill. II. Title.
PS2429.M5N5 1994   93-37281   811'.2—dc20

'Twas the Night Before Christmas

by Clement Clarke Moore

illustrated by Mike Artell

Aladdin Books

Macmillan Publishing Company
New York

Maxwell Macmillan Canada
Toronto

Maxwell Macmillan International
New York   Oxford   Singapore   Sydney

'Twas the night before Christmas,

        when all through the house

not a creature was stirring, not even a mouse.

The stockings were hung by the chimney with care,

in hopes that St. Nicholas soon would be there.

The children were nestled all snug in their beds,
while visions of sugar plums danced in their heads.

And Mama in her kerchief, and I in my cap,
had just settled our brains for a long winter's nap.

When out on the roof there arose such a clatter,
I sprang from my bed to see what was the matter.
Away to the window I flew like a flash,
tore open the shutter, and threw up the sash.

The moon on the breast of the new-fallen snow
gave the lustre of midday to objects below,
when, what to my wondering eyes should appear,
but a miniature sleigh and eight tiny reindeer.

With a little old driver, so lively and quick,
I knew in moment it must be St. Nick.

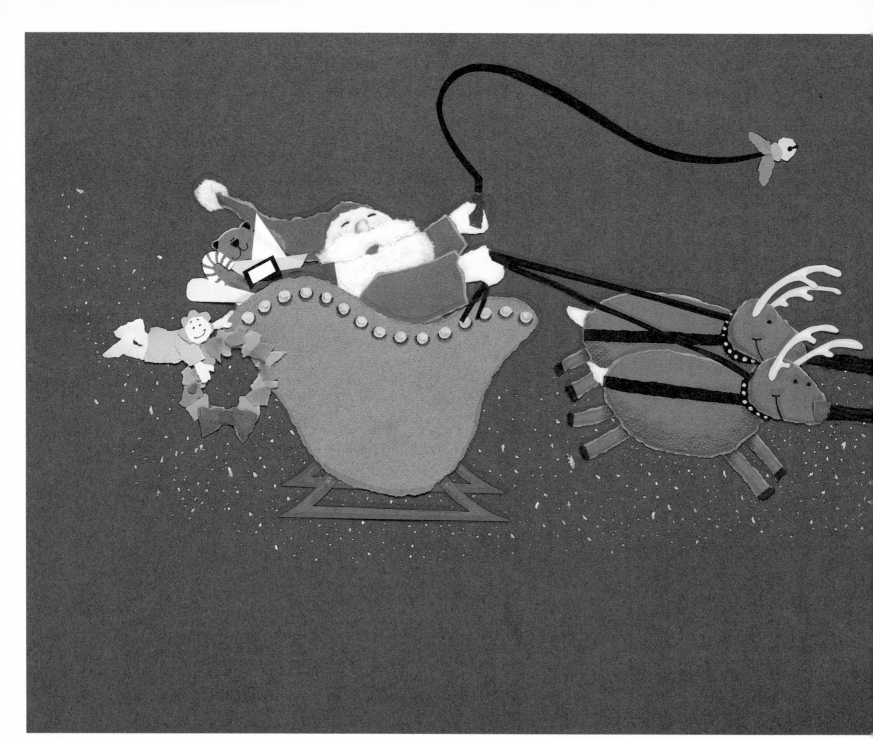

More rapid than eagles
　　his coursers they came,
and he whistled and shouted
　　and called them by name:

"Now, Dasher! Now, Dancer!
　　Now, Prancer and Vixen!
On, Comet! On, Cupid!
　　On, Donner and Blitzen!
To the top of the porch!
　　To the top of the wall!
Now dash away! Dash away!
　　Dash away all!"

As dry leaves that before
the wild hurricane fly,
when they meet with an obstacle,
mount to the sky,
so up to the house-top
the coursers they flew,
with the sleigh full of toys,
and St. Nicholas too.

And then, in a twinkling,
I heard on the roof
the prancing and pawing
of each little hoof.

As I drew in my head and was turning around,
down the chimney St. Nicholas came with a bound.

He was dressed all in fur, from his head to his foot,
and his clothes were all tarnished with ashes and soot.
A bundle of toys he had flung on his back,
and he looked like a peddler just opening his pack.

His eyes—how they twinkled! His dimples, how merry!

His cheeks were like roses, his nose like a cherry!

His droll little mouth was drawn up like a bow,

and the beard of his chin was as white as the snow.

The stump of a pipe he held tight in his teeth,

and the smoke it encircled his head like a wreath.

He had a broad face and a little round belly,

that shook when he laughed, like a bowl full of jelly.

He was chubby and plump, a right jolly old elf,
and I laughed when I saw him, in spite of myself.
A wink of his eye and a twist of his head
soon gave me to know I had nothing to dread.

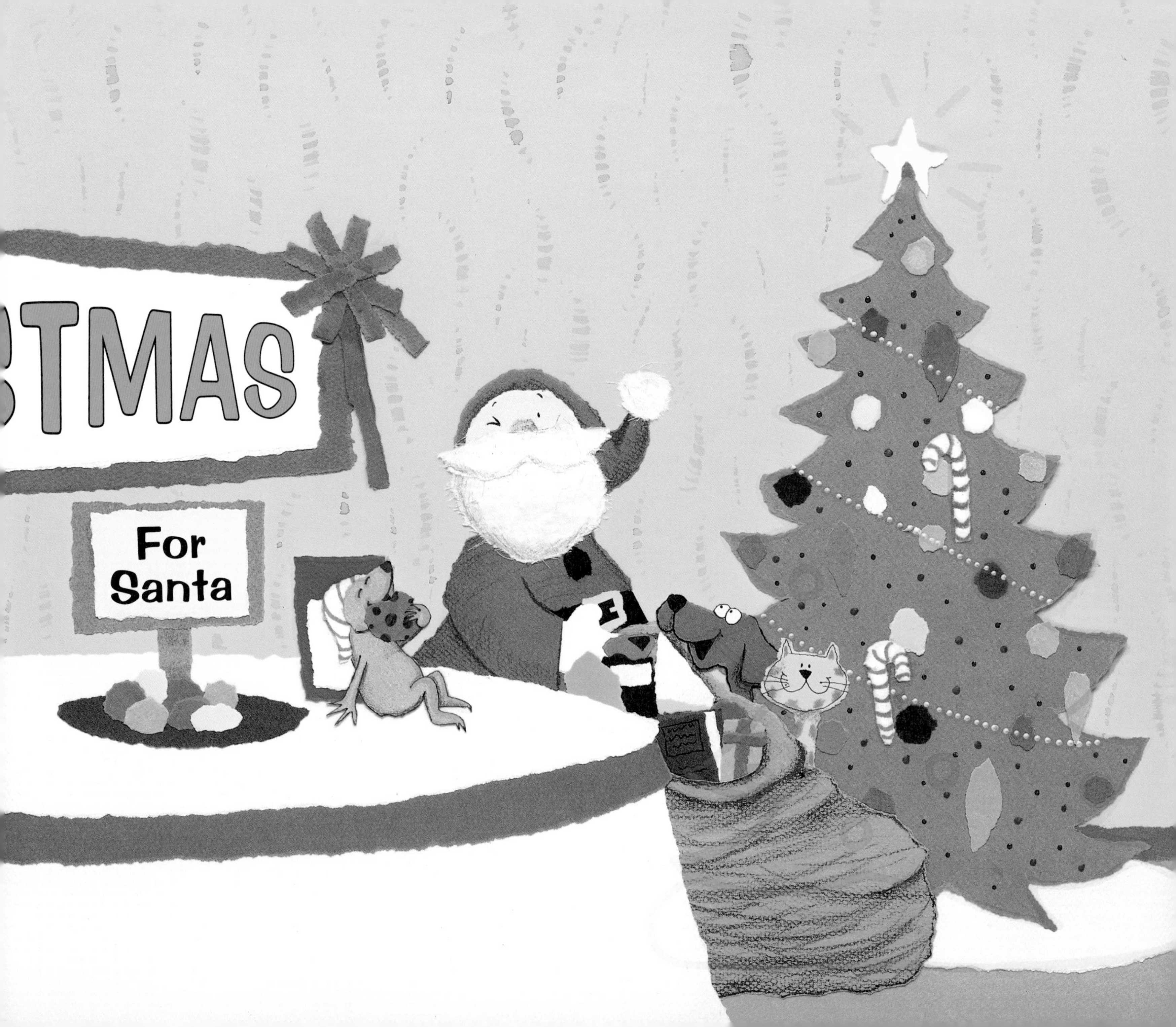
TMAS
For
Santa

He spoke not a word, but went straight to his work,
and filled all the stockings, then turned with a jerk.

And laying his finger aside of his nose,
and giving a nod, up the chimney he rose.

He sprang to his sleigh, to his team gave a whistle,
And away they all flew like the down of a thistle.

But I heard him exclaim,
ere he drove out of sight,

*H*appy Christmas to all, and to all a good night!!

Ho, Ho, Ho!